Gourmet VINEGARS

The How-Tos of Making & Cooking with Vinegars

Marsha Peters Johnson

Previo Ltd
Now Expanded

SIBYL
PUBLICATIONS
Portland, Oregon

Published by SIBYL Publications, Inc. • 1007 S.W. Westwood Drive • Portland, Oregon 97239
(503) 293-8391 • (800) 240-8566 • www.sibylbooks.com

Originally published by Culinary Arts Ltd. 1986, revised 1990. Revised and expanded in 2002 by Sibyl
Publications, Inc.

ISBN: 1-889531-05-7

Graphic Design and Photography: *Design Studio Selby*

6 5 4 3 2 1   Printed in Canada

Cataloging in Publication

    Johnson, Marsha Peters.
      Gourmet vinegars : the how-tos of making & cooking
    with vinegars / Marsha Peters Johnson.
      p. cm. -- (Creative cooking series)
      Includes index.
      "Now revised and expanded."
      ISBN: 1-889531-05-7

      1. Cookery (Vinegar) 2. Vinegar   I. Title.

    TX819.V5J65 2002   641.6'2
                  QB102-200604

From the publisher:

Gourmet Vinegars was previously published by Culinary Arts Ltd. In 1998 Sibyl
Publications purchased all rights to *Gourmet Vinegars, Gourmet Mustards* and
Classic Liqueurs. This presented an exciting opportunity to create a series of
cookbooks on specialty subjects, called **CREATIVE COOKING SERIES**. We will
be expanding into new areas with the latest how-tos on specific foods. If you
have comments or suggestions for upcoming titles, contact Sibyl Publications at
1-800-240-8566 or by email at ms@sibylbooks.com. Call or write for free catalog.

VINEGARS

CONTENTS

Vinegar was probably discovered when the first cask of wine turned sour. The French origin of the word "vinegar" is "vinagre", which means, literally, sour wine.

I discovered vinegars in Europe as I ate my way through thirteen countries one year. Later, finding myself at loose ends, I finally connected the superb Oregon berry crops with an excellent white wine vinegar to start my own business, Oregon's Own Gourmet Vinegars. The success story continued! My company flourished and, by 1986, I had completed negotiations with the prestigious Oregon firm, Heins Honey, for the sale of my business. With Heins' interest in expanding its line to include a broader variety of quality gourmet foods, my vinegars are now reaching a wider market under the label of Oregon Trails Gourmet Vinegars.

Over the years, it has been my pleasure to develop a wide variety of ways to use gourmet vinegars. In this book, you will find my secrets for both making and cooking with the whole range of exciting flavors. I hope you love or learn to love vinegars as much as I do.

Marsha Peters Johnson

"A loaf of bread," the Walrus said,
"Is what we chiefly need,
 Pepper and vinegar besides
 Are very good indeed."
LEWIS CARROLL, *THROUGH THE LOOKING-GLASS*

Basics of VINEGAR MAKING

About Equipment

You will probably be able to find everything you'll need in your own kitchen cupboards. The basic rule in all vinegar making is to avoid any contact between the vinegar and certain metals, such as aluminum or iron. Since vinegar is such an acidic substance, it will leach the metal molecules from a metal pot, bowl or spoon. Be careful to use only plastic or glass bottles for storing and aging the vinegars. In addition, make sure that you have tight-fitting lids for those jugs, jars or bottles as your sweet fruit and spice vinegars can draw "friends" of the unwelcome variety.

Vinegar Making Equipment

Several large ($^1/2$-gallon) plastic tubs for mixing and aging, with
    tight-fitting lids

Plastic spoons

Plastic strainer or colander

Glass or plastic measuring cups: 1-, 2- and 4-cup sizes

Plastic funnel, sized to fit small bottle openings

Cheesecloth or fine cotton cloth for straining

Equipment for Bottling

Bottles or glass jars with lids: 6-, 8-, 12- or 16-ounce size

Screw tops for bottles, metal with plastic liners or plastic lids

Corks for bottles, brand new; please do not use recycled ones

Wax for sealing corks, half paraffin and half beeswax

Labels

Ribbon to run under wax or tie on recipe

Ground spices or oils for mixing with the wax

Preparation of Equipment

Everything needs to be completely free of grease or other contamination before beginning mixing the vinegars. To do this, wash all the items in hot soapy water, then rinse with very hot, almost boiling water. You may also accomplish the same "squeaky-clean" equipment by putting everything through a full dishwasher cycle, which is definitely easier.

Vinegars

Since you won't actually be making the initial vinegar itself, it is important to learn about what varieties are available at your local supermarkets and the vast differences between these types. The following is a list of vinegars commonly found in most cities:

Plain white distilled

Apple cider

Red and white wine

Malt

Rice

Balsamic

Strength of vinegar is very important. The acetic acid content of vinegars varies from 4 to 7 percent, with the standard being 5 percent.

Acetic acid content is also referred to by "grains." For example, a 5% acetic acid content vinegar is also known as a 50-grain vinegar. The whole business refers to the amount of water the vinegar is diluted with; 50-grain vinegar is 5% vinegar, 95% water. The advantage of seeking out a higher acetic acid content is that it helps keep food fresher longer, acting as a better preservative, which is what vinegar really is in the first place. Depending on what the vinegar is made from, it can have many different qualities. White distilled vinegar, in my opinion, has hardly any taste other than sour, and is fine for making certain

things like pickles, where you want only sour. However, if you are seeking the best in vinegars, look to the wine vinegars made from top-quality wines. The taste and body of the grapes will shine through your finished bottles and you will be more satisfied with the results. Read the labels carefully and see if you can determine the vinegar's origin, acidic level and place of manufacture.

I have come to discover that, given a fair chance, any vinegar, excluding distilled white vinegar, can lend a pleasing quality and aroma to a final product. I do enjoy using a strong white wine vinegar for most of my concoctions, but have expanded my taste over the past years to allow room for the slightly pungent, full fruity bouquet of apple cider vinegars. Garlic tends to blend exceptionally well with this staple of the pantry, as well as onion flavors. Don't be afraid to try just about any combination of vinegars, either. Mixing a white wine with an equal part of rice vinegar can be delightful mixed with fresh herbs, a dollop of lovely pale golden green olive oil and seasoned to taste.

The white wine varieties do act as the best base, however, for the showy fresh fruit and vegetable colors that are extracted during aging. For home use and gift-giving, take these factors into your consideration and planning. Balsamic vinegars are still expensive, usually imported and are generally of such a high caliber in flavor that it would be a crime to try to add anything other than good olive oil and seasonings. I have recently acquired some malt vinegars and have had moderate success in playing with additions of nasturtium seeds and flowers, making for a welcome peppery taste that is even good over the traditional fish and chips. Barley vinegar I have not come into close friendship with yet and if you have success with it, please let me know!

Vinegars, in particular the wine varieties, are made from good quality drinking wines. It is not just "good wine gone bad." As a matter of fact, it is nearly impossible to turn out a decent vinegar by letting good wine sour. What you end up with is sour wine, not good vinegar. Vinegar is the result of careful introduction of friendly bacteria into wine, monitored under carefully

controlled temperatures and environment. Homemade vinegars use a "mother" which is rather nasty looking stuff resembling a thick jelly-like material, which, if carefully mixed with wine, will turn out a beautiful vinegar. However, it is a chancy business and you're better off buying the vinegar already made from the store.

Shelf Life of Finished Vinegar

Flavored vinegars will keep up to 18 months, possibly longer, if stored in proper containers in a cool dark place. Some fruit sugars, like strawberry or blueberry, tend to caramelize after a while and turn slightly brown, which isn't as attractive as a clear red or violet liquid. These two vinegars should be used up in 3 months to avoid this problem. Since high-acid content vinegar is often used as a preservative itself, spoiling just isn't a problem. Usually, you'll end up wishing you'd made twice as much because it disappears so quickly.

Bottles

This is the place to use your creative ideas for containers and finishing touches, as long as you avoid any metal containers or lids. Glass bottles or jars, special decanters with plastic lids, rubber rings, glass tops or corks are all appropriate for vinegars when properly scrubbed and sterilized with boiling water. A bottle brush can be handy for cleaning out re-used bottles. You can also use plastic containers if they are of food-grade quality. Of course then you miss out on the treat of seeing the beautiful colors and/or ingredients of the vinegars, which are half the reason for making them!

To use corks for the top, buy only top-quality corks from a winery supply or beer-making supply store and inspect them carefully for signs of decay or imperfection. After inserting them into the bottle mouth, finish by dipping in wax, preferably a mixture of half paraffin to half beeswax for easy peeling later on. The melted wax may be improved by adding ground spices such

as cinnamon or strong oils like oil of cloves. This gives a nice warm tone and scent to the finished product. Then with a ribbon tied around the neck holding a special recipe for that vinegar, you're ready for holiday gift-giving, house-warming or birthday parties.

Fruits, Flavoring Spices, Herbs and Vegetables

In my business I select fresh top-quality berries direct from rich Oregon fields to make my vinegar nectars. In your area the produce available to you may be different. Just remember, buy the best quality produce you can find, as fresh as possible. Frozen produce is also useful and makes good quality vinegars. Most of your spices will be dried. Herbs should be fresh, especially if you plan to leave them in the bottles. Dried herbs are satisfactory but need a little help in heating and straining before bottling. As the quantities of vinegar required for vinegar making are not large, you can supply yourself with a full pantry of specialty flavors for a relatively small investment in raw materials.

Certain fruits and vegetables need to be peeled, chopped, mashed, smashed, blended or heated to release all their flavors into the vinegar. We'll deal with that in the individual recipes for vinegars that follow this chapter.

Aging Time

Some recipes that require heating will be ready for use at once, but the majority of vinegars in this book require about a month to fully develop their unique flavors. I believe in Cold Processing as opposed to Hot Processing. Treating the fruit or herbs gently and combining them with vinegar in its prime makes a great finished product, full of the natural vitamins and nutrients leached from the fruit or herbs during the aging process. Minimum aging times are indicated in the vinegar recipes.

I have called for plastic tubs with tight lids to be used in the aging process. Food-grade quality plastic does not affect the flavor or taste at all and turns out

a very fine vinegar. Glass is also good for aging, such as quart jars, as long as the lid is not metal! The best flavor, however, can be obtained by using wood casks. These can be obtained from wine or beer-making outlets.

Straining

While siphoning works well in certain vinegars, other vinegars need not be strained at all, only bottled at mixing time. However, there are many vinegars which need to be strained several times through double layers of cheesecloth inside a plastic strainer to eliminate fruit/herb/vegetable pieces and leave a perfectly clear, stunningly colored liquid for the bottles.

Using two layers of cheesecloth inside your plastic colander or strainer, pour your aged vinegar mix into the strainer gently, catching the liquid under the strainer in a clean plastic tub or large bowl. You may need to strain several times using clean cheesecloth each time and rinsing the tubs or glass bowls every time until you obtain a perfectly clear liquid.

Equivalent Liquid Measures

3 teaspoons	=	1 tablespoon
2 tablespoons	=	1 ounce
4 tablespoons	=	$^1/_4$ cup
5 $^1/_3$ tablespoons	=	$^1/_3$ cup
8 ounces	=	1 cup
16 tablespoons	=	1 cup
2 cups	=	1 pint
16 ounces	=	1 pint
2 pints	=	1 quart
32 ounces	=	1 quart
4 quarts	=	1 gallon

Metric Conversion

1 milliliter	=	.034 fluid ounces
1 liter	=	33.8 fluid ounces or 4.2 cups
1 fluid ounce	=	29.56 milliliters
1 fluid cup	=	236 milliliters
1 fluid quart	=	946 milliliters or .946 liters
1 teaspoon	=	5 milliliters
1 tablespoon	=	15 milliliters

MAKING
Gourmet
VINEGARS

*T*his chapter will help you set up your own complete pantry of specialty vinegars. Before long, you will be choosing gourmet vinegars to replace regular vinegar or lemon juice in your favorite recipes. The subtle difference will be evident as your barbecue sauces, salad dressings and marinades become tastier. They will add the gourmet touch that is the signature of a truly good cook. People will start asking for your recipes and will be surprised to learn the difference is the vinegar! Do them a favor and give them a bottle of your favorite with the requested recipe attached.

Berry Vinegar

BASIC RECIPE

Of all the fruits, berries are perhaps the easiest to use in vinegar making as they contain so much juice and don't need to be peeled or pitted. Here in Oregon the berries are huge, juicy and perfect for good vinegar. If you can get fresh, so much the better; if not, frozen will do, but be sure to use frozen berries with no sugar added.

Many people ask me what my favorite vinegar is and I always say "Raspberry." Looking through the recipe section of this book made me realize that there are very few foods that wouldn't be enhanced by the addition of this outstanding vinegar. The following basic recipe can be made with any of the berries listed.

MAKES ABOUT 1 QUART

1 to 1^1/2 pounds ripe berries, washed and drained (see below)
1 quart white vinegar*, preferably 5% acidity or higher

In a large glass bowl, prepare berries as indicated below. Stir in the vinegar. Pour into jar/s for aging. (If using more than one jar, be sure to divide berries and vinegar equally.) Cover with plastic wrap secured by rubber bands. Let age in a cool, dark place about 3 to 4 weeks, then strain through cheesecloth and plastic strainer until clear. Pour into bottles and seal. Use within 18 months.

*For the best color effect, use white wine vinegar. You may substitute red wine vinegar for a nice full-bodied taste.

BERRY VARIATIONS

Use any of the following berries in the <u>Basic Recipe</u>:

Blackberries: 1 pound, crushed well
Blueberries: 1 pound, ground in a blender with about ^{1}/3 cup of the vinegar
Cranberries: 1 pound, ground in a blender with about ^{1}/3 cup of the vinegar
Currants: 1 pound fresh, ground in a blender with about ^{1}/3 cup of the
vinegar

Huckleberries: 1 pound, ground in a blender with about $^1/_3$ cup of the vinegar
Loganberries: 1 pound, crushed well
Marionberries: 1 pound, crushed well
Raspberries: 1 to 1$^1/_2$ pounds, crushed well
Strawberries: 1 pound, hulled and crushed well

Fruit Vinegar

BASIC RECIPE

In general, making fruit vinegars takes a little more preparation than herb, spice or berry vinegars. However, the results are quite pleasant and add something to foods that can't be obtained any other way. MAKES ABOUT 1 QUART

>   1 to 2 pounds ripe fruit, washed and drained (see list below)
>   1 quart white or red wine vinegar, 5 to 7% acidity

Combine prepared fruit and vinegar in a large glass bowl. Pour into glass jar/s for aging. (If using more than one jar be sure to divide fruit and vinegar equally.) Store in a cool dark place for at least 1 month to properly age and mellow flavors.

FRUIT VARIATIONS

Use any of the following fruits in the <u>Basic Recipe</u>:

Apricot: 1 pound apricots. Pit but do not peel. Grind in a meat grinder or chop very fine to release juice.
Cherries: 1 pound cherries, pitted and ground in blender with $^1/_3$ cup of the vinegar.
Kiwi: 8 to 9 kiwi fruit, peeled and finely chopped. A very unique color and flavor.

Lemon, Lime or Orange: 3 of any fruit. Thinly peel fruit, being careful not to include the bitter white layer. Finely chop the peel. Squeeze fruit to extract juice and add juice and pulp to vinegar. **TIP**: When bottling, add a few fresh spirals of peel to each final bottle for color.

Nectarine: About 4 to 5 nectarines, pitted. Chop into bits.

Papaya or Mango: 1 large or 2 small fruits. Peel, seed and mash well.

Peach: 1 pound peaches, peeled, pitted and chopped into bits.

Pear: 1 pound pears, peeled, cored and chopped into bits.

Persimmon: 1 pound persimmons, fully ripe and soft. Discard stems, coarsely chop and save juice. Makes about 2 cups of pulp and juice. Gorgeous color.

Pineapple: $1/2$ fresh pineapple. Remove peel, discard. Finely chop fruit. Add any juice to vinegar when mixing.

Rhubarb: 1 pound rhubarb. Finely chop. In saucepan heat rhubarb with $1/4$ cup water until it comes to a boil. Let cool before continuing.

Tangerine: 6 or 7 tangerines. Peel 3 tangerines. Finely chop the peel. Squeeze the juice from all the tangerines. Add the peel, juice and pulp to the vinegar.

Watermelon: About 3 pounds. Remove skin and green rind; discard. Mash remaining watermelon meat, including the seeds. **TIP**: Add a few whole seeds to each final bottle for color.

Herb Vinegar

BASIC RECIPE

Herb vinegars are the most widely distributed and best known vinegars today. Large companies produce them commercially but they are simple and inexpensive to make at home. In my mind's eye, I can see that busy housewife who saw a way to save time and threw a handful of green herbs into the vinegar vat long ago. Lucky us!

M<small>AKES</small> 1 <small>QUART</small>

> 1 generous handful finely chopped fresh herbs* (see list below)
>
> 1 quart good vinegar, any kind with 5% to 7% acidity

Basil (green or purple), chives and flowers, cilantro, dill weed, mint, parsley, rosemary, sage, tarragon, thyme or any other herb you have on hand. Combine herbs and vinegar. Age in covered glass jar/s for 1 month in a cool dark place.

*DRIED HERB VARIATION

You can substitute dried herbs, using 2 to 3 tablespoons per quart. Increase the aging time by 2 weeks. To cut the aging time down to 1 week, gently heat the vinegar and add the dried herbs. Cool, bottle and age as above. Strain through cheesecloth until clear, then bottle.

TIP: Use one or several kinds of herbs as your taste dictates. Some suggestions are **Basil-Mint** or **Dill-Chives**. For a gourmet touch add a sprig of the herb of your choice to the final bottle.

Spice Vinegar

BASIC RECIPE

Perfect for pickles, marinades or coolers. For vinegar in a hurry, use the Hot Process Method to release the essence of the spice immediately. You may prefer, as I do, the slower but simpler Cold Process Method. MAKES 1 QUART

> 1 quart vinegar, any kind
> dried spices, see list below

SPICE VARIATIONS

> 2 to 3 tablespoons whole anise seeds
> 2 to 3 sticks cinnamon
> 2 to 3 tablespoons whole cloves
> 2 to 3 tablespoons peppercorns

Hot Process: Gently heat vinegar in stainless steel pot on the stove-top or in a large glass bowl in the microwave. Add spices to hot vinegar. Cool and strain. Bottle and label at once. (No aging time necessary with this method. Vinegar may be used immediately.)

Cold Process: Put spices into bottles with cool vinegar. Label, then age for 4 weeks before using.

TIP: Add a few whole spices to each final bottle for decoration.

Vegetable Vinegar

BASIC RECIPE

These are perhaps the most unusual vinegars. The flavors are released when the tough fibers are broken down through chopping and mashing. <small>MAKES 1 QUART</small>

    ripe vegetables (see list below)

    1 quart white or red wine vinegar, 5% or 7% acidity

VEGETABLE VARIATIONS

Use <u>one</u> of the following in the <u>Basic Recipe</u>:

    6 to 8 garlic cloves, peeled and mashed flat*

    2 to 3 bunches of green onions, thinly sliced

    1 pound green, red or yellow peppers, seeded and chopped

    3 to 4 hot peppers, seeded and sliced

    $^1/_2$ pound shallots, peeled and chopped

    1 pound sweet onions, peeled and sliced

Prepare vegetables as directed and mix with vinegar. Store in covered jars and age 4 weeks. Remove vegetables by straining through cheesecloth until clear, then bottle.

TIP: Place several pieces of fresh vegetable, such as pepper rings or garlic cloves, in final bottles.

*Option: It is possible to bottle garlic vinegar in one step by adding peeled garlic cloves, cut into halves, to the final bottles with the vinegar.

About Flower Vinegars

Very special are those vinegars that are flavored and colored with flowers. In many other countries, people eat flowers of different varieties, and regard them as casually as you and I would a carrot. If you want to experiment with flowers, do not use those that have been chemically treated for insects, mold or fungus. Also avoid flowers that are near other bushes and plants that have been similarly treated. Of course, do not use poisonous flowers or leaves.

The most common flower vinegar is made using nasturtium flowers, the seed of which is often compared to a caper. You can immerse whole or chopped flowers in vinegar bottles for a stunning effect or combine them with other flavoring agents such as spices, peppers or herbs. Nasturtiums have a peppery taste, which is quite pleasant. Other flowers that you can use include violets, roses, various herb flowers and chive blossoms.

Flower Vinegar
BASIC RECIPE

An impressive and beautiful gift. MAKES I QUART

I quart fine white wine vinegar
I to 2 generous handfuls of flowers, thoroughly washed and drained

Combine in large glass jar and cover tightly. Age 3 months, then strain and use.

About Mixed Vinegars

A mixed vinegar is one made with a combination of flavoring agents that produces a unique and lively blend. To experiment on your own, start with your favorite flavors. After your first taste of success, you will grow bolder and even more creative.

As a general rule of thumb, remember that heat comes ahead of cold. In other words, if one of the ingredients must be heated to release its full flavor and color, do so first and then combine with vinegar. Then add the cold-processed portion and put into plastic containers to age. If more than one ingredient must be heated, do them at the same time. If several or all of the ingredients will be cold-processed, do everything together. It may look like a mixed-up crazy-quilt initially, but given a month of aging time to smooth the flavors, you'll find a treasure after straining.

Sweet Basil with Blueberry Vinegar

Use the purple basil with the purple-violet blueberries for a lovely flavor and color.

MAKES 1 QUART

> 1 quart fine white wine vinegar
> 1 pound fresh or frozen blueberries, pulverized or ground
>   in a blender with $^1/_3$ cup of the vinegar
> 1 good handful of sweet purple basil, leaves and stems,
>   finely chopped

Combine all ingredients. Store in a covered aging container in a cool dark place for 4 weeks. Strain through layers of cheesecloth, then bottle and label. Cap with corks and wax, or use plastic screw-on lids.

TIP: Add a few whole blueberries to final bottle/s for color.

Raspberry Spice Vinegar

This is a wonderful sweet clear red nectar with zip!   MAKES I QUART

- I to I ¹/2 pounds ripe red raspberries
- I quart fine white wine vinegar
- I tablespoons whole cloves, allspice or cracked peppercorns

Mash berries well with wooden spoon. If you prefer, use a blender or food processor, adding ¹/3 cup of the vinegar. Combine berries and vinegar in a large bowl. Add spices and stir well with plastic or wooden spoon. Pour into aging container. Cover, age in a cool dark place for 4 to 6 weeks. Strain through layers of cheesecloth until clear, then bottle and label. Seal with corks dipped in wax or use plastic screw-on caps.

Strawberry with Spice Vinegar

Make strawberry vinegars in small quantities and use them within 3 months as they have a tendency to caramelize and turn a brownish color. Delicious mixed with sour cream and candied ginger as a dip for fresh fruit.   MAKES I QUART

- I pound ripe red strawberries, hulled and mashed
- I teaspoon ground nutmeg
- I quart white or red wine vinegar
- several 2- to 3-inch cinnamon sticks

Mix berries, nutmeg and vinegar together in a large glass bowl. Pour into aging container, adding cinnamon sticks. Seal tightly and age in a cool dark place for 4 weeks. Strain through layers of cheesecloth until clear. Bottle in three to four 6- or 8-ounce glass bottles. Label and cap with corks dipped in wax or plastic screw-on lids.

Apricot with Allspice Vinegar

Pleasingly sweet with a bite of its own, this apricot vinegar is nicely showcased with a touch of spice.   MAKES 1 QUART

- 1 pound ripe juicy apricots, pitted and chopped
- 1 tablespoon whole allspice, slightly crushed
- 1 quart white or red wine vinegar

Combine all ingredients in a large glass bowl. Pour into aging container; seal tightly. Age in a cool dark place for 4 weeks, then strain through layers of cheesecloth until clear. Pour into three to four 6- or 8-ounce glass bottles. Label and cap tightly with corks dipped in wax or plastic screw-on lids.

Peach with Anise Seed Vinegar

A pale salmon-colored vinegar with a slight licorice aroma that is perfect for fruit salad dressings or giving as a gift.   MAKES 1 QUART

- 1 pound ripe peaches, peeled, pitted and chopped
- 1 tablespoon anise seeds, slightly crushed
- 1 quart white wine vinegar

Combine all ingredients in a large bowl, stirring well. Pour into aging container and seal tightly. Age 4 weeks in a cool dark place, then strain through layers of cheesecloth until clear. Pour into three to four 6- or 8-ounce glass bottles. Label and cap tightly with corks dipped in wax or plastic screw-on lids.

Tangerine & Cinnamon Vinegar

A lovely, light orange vinegar with a spicy taste. MAKES 1 QUART

> 6 to 7 tangerines
>
> 1 quart white wine vinegar
>
> 1 tablespoon of your favorite whole spice, such as cinnamon stick, allspice or cloves

Remove and finely chop the tangerine peel. Squeeze pulp to extract juice. Combine vinegar, peel, juice and spice in a large glass bowl. Pour into covered aging container and store in a cool, dark place for 6 weeks. Strain through layers of cheesecloth, then bottle and label. Cap with corks dipped in wax, or use plastic screw-on lids. Label and use within 12 months.

TIP: Add a thin spiral of tangerine peel to each bottle with several whole spices.

Mixed Herbs & Spice Vinegar

Limited only by your imagination. MAKES 1 QUART

> 1 generous handful of your favorite fresh herb
>
> 1 quart fine white or red wine or apple cider vinegar
>
> 1 tablespoon of your favorite dried whole spice, such as allspice, cinnamon stick, cloves or grated fresh ginger root

Finely chop herb. Mix with vinegar and spices in aging container. Seal tightly and age for 4 weeks. Strain through layers of cheesecloth until clear, then bottle and label. Seal with corks dipped in wax, or use plastic screw-on lids.

TIP: Add fresh sprigs of herbs and whole spices as appropriate.

Mint with Clove Vinegar

This spicy cool green vinegar is perfect for marinating leg of lamb or ribs for barbecuing. MAKES 1 QUART

> 1 quart fine white wine vinegar
>
> 1 generous handful of mint leaves and stems, finely chopped, almost puréed
>
> 1 tablespoon of your favorite spices, such as whole cloves, allspice or fresh ground ginger

Combine all ingredients in a large glass bowl. Store in a covered aging container in a cool dark place for 4 weeks. Strain through layers of cheesecloth until clear; then bottle and label. Seal with corks and wax, or use plastic screw-on lids.

TIP: Add a fresh sprig of mint and 1 to 2 whole cloves to final bottles.

Peppers & Spice Vinegar

Sweet bell peppers lend themselves to an addition of spices. This makes a delicious salad dressing vinegar. MAKES 1 QUART

> 2 to 3 large bell peppers, red, green or yellow, seeded, cored and finely chopped or grated
>
> 1 tablespoon allspice, cloves, grated fresh ginger root or a 3-inch stick of cinnamon
>
> 1 quart fine white wine vinegar

Combine all ingredients in a large glass bowl. Pour into a plastic aging container, sealing tightly. Age in a cool dark place for 4 weeks. Strain through layers of cheesecloth until clear, then bottle and label. Seal bottles with corks and wax or plastic screw-on lids.

TIP: Add 1 to 2 whole allspice or cloves and a thin ring of pepper to final bottles.

Chives & Chili Vinegar

A gorgeous vinegar blending the hot taste of peppers with the cool bite of chives.

Makes 1 quart

- 1 quart white or red wine vinegar
- 3 to 4 hot red or green peppers, carefully seeded and coarsely chopped
- 3 to 4 tablespoons minced chives
- 6 to 8 whole chive flowers

Mix vinegar, peppers, minced chives and half of the flowers in a plastic aging container and seal tightly. Age for 4 weeks. Strain through layers of cheesecloth until clear. Place a pepper ring or 2 and 1 or 2 fresh chive flowers in three 8-ounce glass bottles. Fill with strained vinegar. Label and cap with corks dipped in wax or regular plastic screw-on lids.

Green Onions & Peppercorns Vinegar

This delicate green vinegar makes a fine salad dressing. Just add fresh herbs, a dollop of olive oil and a dash of salt.

Makes 1 quart

- 2 to 3 bunches of green onions, washed, trimmed and finely chopped
- 1 tablespoon green peppercorns, crushed
- 1 quart white or red wine vinegar

Combine all ingredients in a large glass bowl. Pour into aging container and seal tightly. Age in cool dark place for 4 weeks. Strain through layers of cheesecloth until clear. Pour into three to four 6- or 8-ounce glass bottles. Label and cap tightly with corks dipped in wax or plastic screw-on lids.

Dilled Garlic Vinegar

This is a very easy recipe for the beginning vinegar maker since the aging and bottling are done in one step. Makes 1 quart

> 6 to 9 whole garlic cloves
>
> sprigs of fresh dill weed, thoroughly washed
>
> 1 quart fine white or red wine vinegar

Cut garlic cloves in half lengthwise. Add 4 to 6 garlic halves and 1 to 2 sprigs dill weed to three 8-ounce bottles. Fill with vinegar; seal with corks and wax or plastic screw-on lids. Label and age 4 weeks before using.

Dilled Onion Vinegar

The full-bodied flavors of onion and dill make this easy-to-prepare vinegar sparkle. Economical to make. Makes 1 quart

> 1 large onion, peeled and sliced into rings about $1/4$-inch thick
>
> sprigs of fresh dill weed, thoroughly washed
>
> 1 quart white or red wine vinegar

Divide onion rings between four 6-ounce bottles. Add 2 to 3 sprigs of dill weed to each bottle and fill with vinegar. Cap with corks dipped in wax or plastic screw-on lids. Label and age for 4 weeks before using.

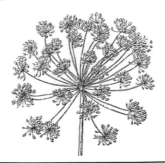

Onion & Peppers Vinegar

Here is a beautiful vinegar to see and smell. The final color depends upon the peppers you choose.
MAKES 1 QUART

> $^3/_4$ pound sweet onion, diced, chopped or sliced into thin rings, with or without skins
>
> 2 to 3 bell peppers: red, yellow or green, seeded, cored and coarsely grated
>
> 1 quart fine white vinegar

Combine all ingredients in a large glass bowl. Pour into aging container. Seal tightly and store in a cool dark place for 4 weeks. Strain through layers of cheesecloth until clear. Pour into glass bottles, seal and label.

TIP: Add a thin onion ring and pepper ring to decorate.

"... four persons are wanted to make a good salad:
　　a spendthrift for oil
　　a miser for vinegar,
　　a counselor for salt,
　　and a madman to stir it all up."
ABRAHAM HAYWARD

COOKING
WITH
Gourmet
VINEGARS

*D*uring the last several years, many people have asked me how I got started with gourmet vinegars. I have thought about this a great deal and there seems to be one simple reason: I love to eat! I have found that vinegar is the secret to better tasting foods.

Vinegar is what I call a "common denominator" ingredient. It can be used in everything from appetizers to drinks. And with the addition of different vinegars you can have an endless variety of flavors.

The recipes that follow were developed from a lifetime of cooking with vinegar, a love of fine food and my culinary curiosity.

TERIYAKI WINGS

Wonderful party or potluck food! Excellent with <u>Sweet Hot Mustard</u>.

Serves 8 as an appetizer

> 1 pound chicken wings (cut off tips and save for stock)
> $^1/_4$ cup soy sauce
> 3 tablespoons brown sugar
> $^1/_2$ teaspoon ground ginger
> 2 to 3 dashes cayenne pepper
> $^1/_4$ cup <u>Orange</u>, <u>Lemon</u> or <u>Garlic Vinegar</u>
> 1 teaspoon lemon juice
> 2 cloves garlic, peeled and mashed

Place wings in shallow pan or ziptop plastic bag. Combine all other ingredients and pour over wings. Marinate in refrigerator overnight. Drain; bake at 300 degrees for 40 minutes.

GARBANZO SMOOTH-AS-SILK DIP

An excellent appetizer or light lunch for those who enjoy nibbling and the flavors of garlic and spices. Serve with fresh rounds of pita or pocket bread, grilled chicken breasts brushed with garlic butter and a simple salad of diced tomato with cucumber coins. MAKES ABOUT 4 CUPS

2 (15 ^{1}/2-ounce) cans garbanzos or chick-peas, well-drained

^{1}/4 cup lemon juice

^{1}/4 cup <u>Orange</u> or <u>Lemon Vinegar</u>

3 cloves garlic, sliced

3 scallions or green onions, sliced

^{1}/2 cup olive oil

1 teaspoon salt

1 teaspoon white pepper

^{1}/2 teaspoon dry mustard

^{1}/2 teaspoon paprika

^{1}/4 teaspoon cumin

Mix everything in a blender and whiz until absolutely smooth as silk. Chill in refrigerator overnight to bring out flavors.

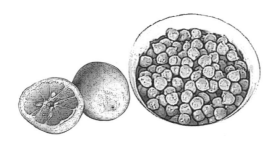

CHINESE STYLE HOT 'N' SOUR SOUP

This is a delicious way to start an Oriental feast, especially when paired with grilled marinated fish fillets and cucumber salad. MAKES 6 LARGE OR 8 MEDIUM-SIZED SERVINGS

$1/4$ pound sliced lean pork steak

2 tablespoons soy sauce

2 tablespoons granulated sugar

1 teaspoon fresh peeled minced ginger root

2 tablespoons peanut oil

$1/2$ cup sliced fresh mushrooms

1 cup drained bamboo shoots

1 pound drained tofu, cubed

6 cups chicken broth, fat skimmed off

$3/4$ cup Garlic, Onion & Peppers or Green Onions & Peppercorns Vinegar

$1/2$ cup soy sauce

3 tablespoons cornstarch

salt and pepper to taste

2 eggs, beaten slightly

sliced green onions, as garnish

Marinate pork in soy sauce, sugar and ginger root for 15 minutes. Drain well, then sauté pork in oil over high heat in a large wok or saucepan until just cooked. Add mushrooms and shoots. Stir over heat 2 to 3 minutes. Then add tofu, chicken broth, vinegar and soy sauce. Combine cornstarch with a little water. Add to soup and bring to boil, stirring until thickened. Reduce to a simmer and correct seasonings with salt and pepper. Add beaten eggs slowly, stirring in well to make the "soup flowers." Serve hot in bowl, floating sliced green onions on top.

GARLIC FESTIVAL GAZPACHO WITH GARLIC VINEGAR

This chilled soup was served at The Ark Garlic Festival in Nahcotta, Washington and was a hit with all the garlic-lovers on that hot June afternoon.   SERVES 8

3 large tomatoes, seeded and chopped

I green pepper, seeded and chopped

I red (sweet) pepper, seeded and chopped

I medium cucumber, peeled and chopped

I cup finely chopped celery

$^1/_2$ cup minced green onion

2 avocados, seeded, peeled and diced

4 cups unsalted tomato juice

3 tablespoons olive oil

5 tablespoons Garlic Vinegar

2 cloves garlic, minced

2 teaspoons salt

$^1/_2$ teaspoon black pepper

dash cayenne pepper, if desired

sour cream, for garnish

Mix all ingredients, except sour cream, in a large plastic or glass container. Chill overnight. Serve in large bowls or mugs; garnish with a dollop of sour cream.

OREGON BLUEBERRY CHICKEN

This was the first recipe I developed using our <u>Blueberry Vinegar</u> and it is so exceptional that it alone is responsible for the continuing success of the business. People will mention to me months after I've served it at a demonstration how much they loved "that chicken."   SERVES 4

> 4 split-boned chicken breasts (or unboned if you prefer)
> 2 tablespoons butter
> ^{1}/4 cup chopped onion
> 4 tablespoons <u>Blueberry Vinegar</u>
> ^{1}/4 cup chicken stock
> ^{1}/4 cup sour cream
> 1 tablespoon chopped tomato
> fresh blueberries, for garnish

Sauté chicken in butter on higher heat until golden, about 3 minutes on each side, longer if unboned. Remove chicken from pan and set aside. Reduce heat and add onion; cook until transparent, about 5 minutes. Add vinegar and raise heat until sauce is reduced to a spoonful. Whisk in stock, sour cream and tomato, simmering over lower heat for 1 minute. Return chicken to pan and simmer until well cooked, about 8 to 10 minutes. Serve at once garnished with blueberries.

VARIATION

Oregon Blueberry Chicken Crêpes

SERVES 4 ELEGANTLY

Prepare <u>Oregon Blueberry Chicken</u> as directed, with these changes. Slice the uncooked chicken breasts into small slivers. Increase stock to $^1/2$ cup. Increase sour cream to $^3/4$ cup. Increase chopped tomato to $^1/4$ cup.

   Prepare I dozen crêpes. Divide cooked chicken evenly between crêpes and roll up. Place in flat, oven-proof serving dish. Pour remaining sauce over the top and bake at 350 degrees for 20 minutes. Garnish with fresh blueberries and additional sour cream just before serving.

CHINESE CHICKEN

A regular family favorite served with brown rice and <u>Creamy Cucumber Salad</u>. SERVES 4

   4 chicken breasts, boned and cubed
   2 tablespoons butter
   I (20-ounce) can pineapple tidbits, drained, save juice
   $^1/3$ cup <u>Green Pepper</u> or <u>Raspberry Vinegar</u>
   2 tablespoons cornstarch, mixed with a little water
   $^1/3$ cup brown sugar
   I tablespoon honey
   2 tablespoons soy sauce
   I green bell pepper
   I red bell pepper

Sauté chicken in butter until browned and cooked through. Keep warm. In a pot combine saved juice, vinegar, cornstarch with water, sugar, honey and soy sauce. Cook over medium heat, stirring until thickened. Seed and slice peppers. Add pineapple, peppers and chicken to the sauce. Serve over rice.

INCREDIBLE LIME CHICKEN

Delicious served with steamed rice or pasta al dente.   SERVES 4 TO 6

  4 to 6 boneless chicken breasts, pounded slightly to flatten

  3 tablespoons margarine or butter

  $^1/_2$ cup onion, minced

  2 cloves garlic, minced

  I lime, squeezed and thin green rind scraped into the juice

  3 tablespoons <u>Lime Vinegar</u>

  $^1/_4$ cup chicken stock (to make, boil bones from breasts in water to cover for 20 minutes, strain and cool)

  salt and white pepper to taste

In large skillet, sauté onions and garlic in melted margarine over medium heat for about 3 minutes. Add chicken breasts and brown on both sides, turning once, for about 8 minutes total.

   Mix lime juice, vinegar and stock; pour over breasts, turning to coat well. Simmer gently about 5 more minutes until cooked through. Remove breasts to serving platter. Turn up heat and boil sauce in pan, stirring vigorously to scrape up bits on bottom of pan, for about 3 minutes. Season sauce to taste with salt and white pepper. Pour over breasts and serve at once.

SPICY TENDER CHICKEN BREASTS

Delicious with rice, refried beans and salad.   Serves 6

> 6 boneless chicken breasts
>
> 2 tablespoons <u>Garlic</u> or other flavor <u>Vinegar</u>
>
> $^1/_2$ cup mayonnaise
>
> $^1/_2$ cup thick spicy salsa, medium hot, or as you prefer

Place chicken in baking pan that has been sprayed with vegetable oil. Sprinkle with vinegar and let sit for 20 minutes. Mix salsa with mayonnaise; spread over chicken.

Cover and bake at 350 degrees for 25 minutes or until cooked through.

EXTRA GARLICKY CHICKEN WITH SAUCE

Perfect with rice or pasta, plus salad or fresh steamed green beans.   SERVES 4

  4 boneless chicken breasts
  2 tablespoons butter
  4 cloves garlic, minced
  $^1/_2$ cup minced onion
  dash of ginger powder
  salt and pepper
  1 cup white wine
  $^1/_3$ cup <u>Basil</u> or other flavor <u>Vinegar</u>
  $^1/_2$ cup heavy cream
  $^1/_2$ cup sour cream

Sauté chicken, garlic, onion and ginger powder in butter over medium-high heat until brown on all sides. Sprinkle with salt and pepper. Pour over white wine and vinegar; sauté about 15 minutes over medium heat until completely cooked.

  Remove chicken to serving plate and keep warm. Stir up juices in pan; add cream and sour cream. Stir well about 2 minutes until warm and thickened but not boiling. Pour over chicken and serve.

RASPBERRY SEAFOOD SAUTÉ

An elegant, simple dish to show off your beautiful clear red <u>Raspberry Vinegar</u>. Serve with buttered noodles or rice. Serves 4

- $^{1}/_{4}$ cup minced onion
- 2 tablespoons butter
- 3 tablespoons <u>Raspberry Vinegar</u>
- $^{1}/_{4}$ cup vegetable or fish stock
- 8 ounces fresh tiny shrimp, cooked
- 8 ounces fresh scallops
- $^{1}/_{4}$ cup sour cream
- 1 tablespoon diced tomato
- fresh raspberries, as garnish

In a large skillet or wok, sauté onion in butter until transparent, about 3 to 4 minutes. Add vinegar, stock, shrimp and scallops and cook briefly, about 5 minutes, stirring often. Scallops should be opaque. Stir in sour cream over low heat; add tomato at the last minute. Serve at once. Garnish with fresh raspberries, if desired.

SNAPPY FISH DISH

A wonderfully quick way to prepare fish in a healthy, low-fat style.   SERVES 2

1 pound thin boneless white fish, like sole
1/2 pound mung bean sprouts, fresh
1/4 cup any flavor <u>Vinegar</u>
1 tomato, chopped
1 onion, chopped
1 clove garlic, minced
2 celery ribs, chopped
1/2 green pepper, diced or 1 (4-ounce) can diced green chilies,
     mild or hot variety, depending on your taste
1 teaspoon chili powder
1/2 teaspoon salt
3 tablespoons olive oil
dash cayenne pepper, if desired

Place fish into flat microwaveable pan. Top with sprouts. Mix other ingredients well to make a fresh salsa mixture, seasoning to taste for a mild or spicy hot version. You may add a dash of cayenne pepper, if you wish. Use 1 cup of salsa to pour over top of sprouts. Cover with plastic microwave wrap, leaving a tiny vent hole at one corner. Microwave on high for 3 minutes, turning once half-way through. Fish is cooked when it is solid white all the way through, which may required an additional minute on high. Garnish with any remaining salsa.

LEMON HERB FISH FILLETS

Light and summery, serve with fresh tomato salad and garlic bread.   <small>SERVES</small> 6

- 1 box herbed stuffing mix
- 2 garlic cloves, minced
- $^1/_3$ cup grated Parmesan cheese
- 1 teaspoon dill weed
- 2 teaspoons lemon juice
- 2 tablespoons <u>Dill</u> or other flavor <u>Vinegar</u>
- $^1/_2$ teaspoon black pepper
- $^1/_3$ cup melted butter
- 3 pounds firm fish fillets, such as salmon

Mix stuffing, garlic, cheese, dill, lemon juice, vinegar and pepper. Blend in half of the melted butter and stir well. Place fish fillets in greased glass baking pan; pour over remaining butter. Then cover with stuffing. Bake at 350 degrees for 20 to 25 minutes or until fish flakes when pierced with a fork.

SPECIAL SPANISH RICE

This dish represents all the warm homey cooking you remember from childhood. This easy recipe uses vinegar to enliven the overtones of tomato.   SERVES 8

 2 pounds ground beef, browned and drained
 2 medium sweet onions, chopped
 2 green bell peppers, seeded and chopped
 1 red bell pepper, seeded and chopped
 1 (28-ounce) can tomatoes
 1 (8-ounce) can herbed tomato sauce
 1 cup water
 2 teaspoons chili powder, less for a milder rice
 2 teaspoons salt or to taste
 1 teaspoon cumin
 2 teaspoons Worcestershire sauce
 ⅓ cup <u>Peppers & Spice</u>, <u>Blackberry</u>, <u>Rosemary</u> or <u>Cherry Vinegar</u>
 1 cup uncooked brown rice

Combine all ingredients in a large oven-proof baking dish. Bake for 1 hour at 350 degrees.

TIP: This dish can also be frozen after cooking and reheated for 30 minutes at 350 degrees.

TENDER BEEF WITH MUSHROOMS

I like to prepare food that is easy but tastes like I spent all day in the kitchen, don't you? This recipe is a good example. Team it with fresh pasta and French bread for a dinner that is company-perfect.
SERVES 6

2 pounds cubed stew beef, trimmed of fat

2 sweet onions, sliced

2 tablespoons brown sugar

2 cups sliced mushrooms

1 cup beef stock

$^1/_2$ cup <u>Garlic</u>, <u>Thyme</u> or <u>Blueberry Vinegar</u>

1 cup sour cream

sliced green onions and chopped parsley, as garnish

Combine all ingredients except sour cream and garnish. Place in Dutch oven. Bake at 300 degrees for 1 $^1/_2$ hours until beef is fork-tender. Remove from heat and stir in sour cream. Place in attractive serving dish and garnish.

EASY HAM WITH FRUIT

On a cool fall or winter evening, this recipe will fill your entire house with a marvelous aroma, drawing you into the kitchen like magic. Serve with brown rice.

MAKES 6 SERVINGS

2 to 2¹/₂ pounds boneless ham, preferably smoked

2 cups water

I teaspoon ground cloves

2 green onions, chopped

I2 pitted prunes

I carrot, scraped and sliced

I teaspoon black pepper

¹/₂ cup <u>Raspberry</u>, <u>Peach with Anise Seed</u>, <u>Shallot</u> or <u>Mango Vinegar</u>

Put ham into Dutch oven. Mix all other ingredients in large bowl and pour over ham. Bake at 300 degrees for 2 hours.

DELICIOUS HAM STEAKS

Serve with rice, pasta or scalloped potatoes.

SERVES 4

4 big ham steaks (about 6 to 8 ounces each), with bone in center

¹/₂ cup brown sugar

2 teaspoons Dijon mustard

I to 2 tablespoons <u>Blackberry</u> or other flavor <u>Vinegar</u>

Place ham steaks in baking pan. Mix brown sugar, mustard and vinegar in a bowl; spread evenly over ham steaks. Cover pan with foil and bake at 350 degrees for 20 to 25 minutes until heated through.

RASPBERRY PORK CHOPS

*This recipe is on the label of my **Oregon Raspberry Vinegar**. When you taste it, you'll know why.*

SERVES 4

> 4 lean pork chops
> 2 tablespoons flour, if desired
> 1 1/2 tablespoons butter
> 1 tablespoon oil
> 6 tablespoons Raspberry Vinegar
> 3/4 cup chicken broth
> 1/2 cup heavy cream

Coat chops with flour, if desired. In skillet, brown chops in butter and oil, turning once. Remove chops; add vinegar and broth to pan drippings. Stir over low heat until well combined. Return chops to pan. Simmer until cooked, about 10 minutes each side. Remove pork to a serving platter. Raise heat and boil sauce until thickened slightly, about 5 minutes. Add cream, stirring until thick. Pour over pork chops and serve at once.

VARIATION

Raspberry Chicken

Follow the recipe above except use 4 split-boned chicken breasts instead of pork chops.

*For flavorful make-your-own mustards, see **Gourmet Mustards: The How-Tos of Making & Cooking with Mustards** by Helene Sawyer and Cheryl Long. Easy instructions for making over 42 different mustards. Plus delectable recipes adding that zippy mustard flavor.

MARINATED PORK ROAST WITH HERBS

Easy to make, but an impressive roast to grace a special table. Serve with oven-roasted potatoes.   Serves 8 generously

    2 teaspoons fresh tarragon or 1 teaspoon dried
    1 tablespoon fresh parsley or 1 teaspoon dried
    3 tablespoons crushed dried black peppercorns, divided
    1/2 cup Raspberry, Green Onions & Peppercorns or
        Mixed Herbs & Spice Vinegar
    1/4 cup soy sauce
    3/4 cup red table wine
    1/4 cup water, as necessary
    4- to 5-pound pork roast (center loin cut, as lean as possible)
    2 tablespoons mustard*

Combine herbs, 1 tablespoon of peppercorns, vinegar, soy sauce, wine and water in a shallow dish or a large ziptop plastic bag. Place roast in marinade, turning well. Refrigerate for 8 hours. Turn occasionally. Drain and reserve marinade.

Preheat oven to 325 degrees. Spread mustard over roast and pat on remaining peppercorns. Put in pan in the oven and pour reserved marinade around sides. Bake until meat thermometer reads 170 degrees (3 to 4 hours).

MARINATED FRESH VEGETABLES

Transform fresh vegetables with this exciting marinade. Serves 4 to 6

$^3/_4$ cup salad oil, preferably safflower

$^1/_2$ cup any flavored <u>Vinegar</u>

2 tablespoons lemon juice (omit if you use <u>Lemon Vinegar</u>)

3 tablespoons finely chopped sweet onion

I teaspoon dried tarragon

I teaspoon salt or salt substitute

$^1/_2$ tablespoon granulated sugar, if desired (omit if using a sweet fruit vinegar, like <u>Blackberry Vinegar</u>)

3 to 4 cups cut-up fresh vegetables such as carrots, onion rings, zucchini, cherry tomatoes, pea pods, celery slices, diced sun chokes, broccoli, cauliflower, celery root and olives

Mix all ingredients except vegetables in a bowl using a whisk. Pour marinade over fresh vegetables in flat shallow container. Cover and marinate for at least 3 hours or overnight. Drain and serve.

CARROTS SAUTÉED IN BLACKBERRY VINEGAR

*This simple recipe is so outstanding that I put it on the label of my **Oregon Blackberry Vinegar**. You'll never believe how sweet these carrots are!*　　　SERVES 4 TO 6

4 tablespoons butter

1 cup chopped onion

2 pounds carrots, peeled and sliced into "pennies"

1/3 cup Blackberry Vinegar

1/4 cup chicken stock

Sauté onion in butter, about 5 minutes, until transparent. Add carrots, cover and cook until tender over low heat, about 20 minutes. Add vinegar and stock. Raise heat and stir until liquid evaporates. Serve at once.

GRILLED SWEET PEPPERS

This colorful but simple recipe has enough personality to stand alone as a side dish but is excellent topping sausages or hamburgers.　　　SERVES 8 AS A RELISH

2 red bell peppers

2 green bell peppers

2 sweet yellow peppers

2 to 3 tablespoons olive oil

sprinkle of salt

2 to 3 tablespoons fresh cilantro or basil

1/4 cup Mixed Herbs or Raspberry Vinegar

Seed and chop peppers into large pieces. Place in oven-proof dish. Heat oven to 425 degrees. Mix oil, salt, herb and vinegar together and pour over peppers. Place in oven for about 20 minutes. Serve hot.

GREAT CREAMY CHILLED BROCCOLI

Flavor plus the unexpected combination of crunchiness and creaminess.   SERVES 4

   1 ¹/₂ to 2 pounds broccoli, stalks peeled, trimmed and cut into
      bite-sized pieces
   ¹/₄ cup any flavor <u>Vinegar</u>
   ¹/₄ cup mayonnaise OR salad dressing
   ¹/₂ cup plain yogurt
   ¹/₄ cup sour cream
   2 to 3 green onions, white and green part, thinly sliced
   I can water chestnuts, sliced and drained
   ¹/₂ teaspoon salt
   ¹/₂ teaspoon white pepper

Steam broccoli or cook in microwave until just tender. Immediately put into strainer and run under cold water until cooled. Drain well.

   In large serving bowl, mix other ingredients together, tasting to season properly and pour over broccoli. Cover tightly and chill in refrigerator overnight or at least 4 hours. Turn to coat broccoli well before serving.

Option: Crumble 3 to 4 slices crisp cooked bacon over top just before serving, or 2 diced hard-cooked eggs.

RED APPLE CABBAGE

Hearty winter fare made to go with sliced sweet ham and mustard sauce.   SERVES 6

    2 teaspoons salt or less to taste
    I cup hot chicken broth
    I tablespoon honey
    ^{1}/2 cup <u>Blueberry</u>, <u>Mixed Herbs</u> or <u>Basil Vinegar</u>
    3 tablespoons butter
    I small head red cabbage, thinly sliced
    I yellow onion, thinly sliced
    3 firm red apples, cored and sliced
    sour cream, for garnish

Combine salt, broth, honey, vinegar and butter in large pot. Bring to a simmer, then add cabbage, onion and apples. Stir well and simmer slowly 25 minutes. Garnish with sour cream just before serving.

TOO MANY GREEN BEANS IN THE GARDEN SALAD!

Serve with fresh whole grain bread or whole wheat bread sticks.   SERVES 4 TO 6

  2 pounds thin young ripe green beans, de-stemmed and
      snapped into 2-inch lengths

  $^1/_4$ cup any flavor <u>Vinegar</u>

  I clove garlic, minced

  $^1/_3$ cup olive oil

  2 to 3 tablespoons fresh chopped basil or parsley

  I teaspoon salt

  $^1/_4$ teaspoon fresh black pepper

  3 to 4 slices crisp cooked bacon, crumbled

Steam green beans in stove-top steamer or in microwave until just tender to bite. Rinse at once in cold running water, using a strainer, until cool to touch. Combine other ingredients, except bacon, and mix well with wire whip until blended. Add green beans and toss to coat. Cover and chill in refrigerator for 4 hours or overnight. Serve topped with bacon.

VARIATION

For a complete light entrée, add a can of drained garbanzo beans or a can of drained, rinsed kidney beans and mix well.

CURRIED CHICKEN SALAD

In hot weather this salad is the answer for a cool dinner. Team it up with a spoonful of chutney and fresh fruit for an easy but elegant meal.   SERVES 4

>   2 cups diced cooked chicken or turkey
>   2 cups thinly sliced celery
>   1 (8-ounce) can sliced water chestnuts, drained
>   1 (20-ounce) can pineapple tidbits, drained
>   1 cup mayonnaise
>   2 teaspoons curry powder
>   1 tablespoon soy sauce
>   2 tablespoons <u>Tangerine</u>, <u>Blueberry</u>, or <u>Mixed Herbs & Spice Vinegar</u>
>   shredded lettuce or pita bread

Combine all ingredients, stirring well. Chill for several hours to blend flavors. Serve on a bed of shredded lettuce or as a filling for pita bread.

VALERIE'S SUMMER RICE SALAD

A close friend of mine, a strict vegetarian, created this popular potluck dish. Serves 6

    3 cups cooked brown rice
    $^1/_4$ cup Raspberry or other Vinegar
    about 2 tablespoons fresh basil, dill or tarragon*
    $^1/_3$ cup chopped celery
    3 green onions, chopped
    $^1/_2$ cup sliced black olives
    I cup tiny peas, fresh or frozen
    $^1/_2$ cup carrots, sliced and briefly cooked
    I cup sour cream
    shredded lettuce

Combine cooled rice, vinegar and herb of choice, stirring well. Add remaining ingredients and serve chilled on a bed of lettuce.

*Option: If you have to substitute dried herbs for fresh, use about 2 teaspoons.

CAULIFLOWER SALAD WITH SHRIMP

The use of highly colored fruit vinegar gives a nice pink tint to this salad.

SERVES 4 TO 6

I head cauliflower, finely chopped
I cup thinly sliced celery
2 tablespoons diced onion
2 tablespoons Raspberry, Cranberry or Blackberry Vinegar
$^{1}/_{2}$ cup mayonnaise
salt and pepper
12 ounces fresh tiny cooked shrimp
2 to 3 hard-boiled eggs, as garnish

Combine all ingredients except shrimp and eggs. Chill overnight in refrigerator. Just before serving, stir in shrimp. Garnish with quartered hard-boiled eggs.

TIP: As additional garnish, if desired, mix equal quantities of mayonnaise and whipped cream. Place a dollop on top of each serving.

CREAMY CUCUMBER SALAD

This smooth, creamy dish is Scandinavian in origin. Perfect with baked fish, such as fresh Pacific Ocean salmon. SERVES 4

> 2 cucumbers, peeled and sliced
> 1 teaspoon salt
> 1 cup sour cream
> 3 tablespoons <u>Blackberry</u>, <u>Dilled Garlic</u>, <u>Green Pepper</u> or <u>Rosemary Vinegar</u>
> 4 teaspoons minced green onions

Sprinkle cucumbers with salt in colander and allow to drain for one hour. Rinse with clear water and drain 5 minutes. Mix sour cream, vinegar and onions in serving bowl. Add cucumber slices and refrigerate 2 to 3 hours before serving.

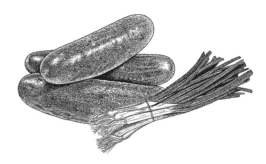

POPEYE'S FAVORITE GREEN SALAD

A delicious salad any time of year and a potluck favorite. Serve in a glass salad bowl to show off the colors.   SERVES 8 TO 10

1 bunch spinach, washed and dried, then either torn
   or sliced into small pieces
1/2 head iceberg lettuce, torn into pieces
1 head butter lettuce, torn into pieces
1 red or white salad onion, sliced into thin rings
1 red pepper, seeded and diced
1 carrot, peeled and sliced into thin sticks
1 (11-ounce) can mandarin oranges, drained
1 (8-ounce) can water chestnuts, whole or sliced, drained
4 to 6 slices crisp cooked bacon, crumbled
2 hard-boiled eggs, chopped
1/2 cup grated Monterey Jack cheese

Dressing:

1/3 cup any flavor <u>Vinegar</u>
1/2 cup olive oil
1 teaspoon Dijon mustard
1 tablespoon honey
salt and pepper to taste

In large salad bowl, combine all vegetables, oranges and water chestnuts, and toss well. In a jar, combine vinegar, oil, mustard, honey, salt and pepper. Shake well to mix. Just before serving, pour over salad and toss well. Sprinkle bacon, eggs and cheese on top or place in bowls on table and let people top their own serving.

COOL AND CREAMY BEET SALAD

*Perfect for a nice spring or summer luncheon. Serve with rye bread or hot garlic
bread fingers.*   Serves 4

  2 (15-ounce) cans whole beets, drained well
  ^{1}/3 cup any flavor <u>Vinegar</u>
  1 clove garlic, minced
  2 tablespoons olive oil
  3 green onions, thinly sliced
  1 peeled cucumber, seeded and diced
  2 hard-boiled eggs, diced
  ^{1}/2 cup mayonnaise
  ^{1}/2 plain yogurt
  ^{1}/2 teaspoon salt
  ^{1}/4 teaspoon pepper
  cabbage, finely chopped

Mix beets with vinegar, garlic and olive oil; let marinate in refrigerator overnight
in a covered container. Just before serving, combine onions, cucumber, eggs,
mayonnaise, yogurt, salt and pepper; fold into beets. Serve on a bed of finely
chopped cabbage.

VERY POSH MARINATED POTATO DINNER SALAD

Unique colors and textures elevate this salad to the main attraction.   SERVES 6 TO 8

2 pounds tiny red, white or yellow potatoes, steamed until just tender
1 (6-ounce) can pitted black olives, drained
1 (14-ounce) can artichoke hearts, drained and chopped
1 salad onion, sliced into thin rings
1 red bell pepper, seeded and diced
1 yellow pepper, seeded and diced
2 to 3 hard-boiled eggs, diced (can omit yolks, if desired)
1 cup diced celery or jicama, peeled and diced
1 firm red tomato, seeded and diced
lettuce leaves, torn into pieces, or red cabbage, finely chopped

Dressing:

$1/2$ cup any flavor Vinegar
$1/2$ cup salad oil (can be part olive oil)
salt and pepper to taste

Combine dressing ingredients and toss with potatoes. Cover and refrigerate for several hours, turning once to coat. Or put potatoes and dressing into a ziptop plastic bag and turn over a couple of times to marinate well.

Remove from refrigerator. Just before serving add rest of salad ingredients, except lettuce or cabbage. Toss well and serve over a bed of lettuce leaves or red cabbage for color.

Option: Add 1 cup diced ham or cheese.

STEAK SALAD WITH RASPBERRY DRESSING

If you are trying to impress that special person in your life, this salad could do the trick. Add fresh French bread, unsalted butter, a good wine and forget dessert! You won't miss it.   SERVES 4

¹/₂ cup oil, part olive
¹/₄ cup <u>Raspberry Vinegar</u>
¹/₄ cup light cream or half-and-half (dieters: use 2% milk)
sprinkle of seasoning salt
1 egg yolk
1 teaspoon mustard
1 teaspoon fresh chopped tarragon or ¹/₄ teaspoon dried
¹/₂ head leaf lettuce, torn into bite-sized pieces
12 ounces thinly sliced cooked steak, medium rare
2 green onions, sliced, as garnish

In top of double boiler combine oil, vinegar, cream, salt, egg yolk, mustard and tarragon. Whisk together over medium heat until thick. This can be done the night before as it must be cold for the salad. Keep in refrigerator.

Place lettuce leaves on 4 plates, then put steak slices on top. Sprinkle with dressing and garnish with green onions.

SPINACH FETTUCCINE SALAD

This makes quite a bit of salad but will keep for several days. The recipe can easily be cut in half. SERVES 8 TO 10

1 ¹/₂ pounds fresh spinach fettuccine
¹/₂ cup oil, part olive oil
¹/₂ cup <u>Garlic</u>, <u>Basil</u> or <u>Chives & Chili Vinegar</u>
2 tablespoons chopped fresh basil
2 cloves fresh garlic, minced
¹/₂ cup chopped fresh parsley
1 (16-ounce) can red beans, drained and rinsed
2 carrots, peeled and chopped
1 sweet onion, diced
2 hard-boiled eggs, chopped

Cook pasta as directed. Drain and rinse with cool water. Mix oil, vinegar, basil, garlic and parsley in a bowl, stirring well. Add pasta, beans, carrots, onion and eggs; toss well. Chill several hours before serving.

ONE OF THE BEST PASTA SALADS FROM MEXICO

My parents love to get away from the Oregon rain when it is at its worst in mid-winter and head down to the warm climate of Mexico for a chance to see the sun. This spicy recipe came back with them. SERVES 6 GENEROUSLY

2 cups uncooked small pasta shells
$^3/4$ cup mayonnaise
$^1/2$ cup salsa or taco sauce
$^1/4$ cup Garlic Vinegar
2 teaspoons onion salt
1 teaspoon chili powder
4 to 5 drops of Tabasco or red pepper sauce
2 cloves of garlic, minced
1 (16-ounce) can of kidney beans, drained
$^1/2$ cup sliced black olives

Cook pasta as directed, drain and rinse. Mix mayonnaise, salsa or taco sauce, vinegar, onion salt, chili powder, hot sauce and garlic. Add pasta, beans and olives; stir well. Chill overnight or for at least 3 hours before serving.

MARINATED MUSHROOMS

For mushroom lovers this can be heaven on earth. Don't be afraid to substitute other mushroom varieties such as chanterelles. SERVES 8 AS AN APPETIZER, 4 AS A SIDE DISH

- I pound mushrooms, cleaned and sliced $^1/_4$-inch thick
- I sweet onion, thinly sliced
- 2 cloves garlic, minced
- I teaspoon dry mustard
- I teaspoon salt
- I tablespoon granulated sugar, if desired
- $^1/_4$ cup water
- $^1/_2$ cup <u>Onion & Peppers</u>, <u>Chives & Chili</u>, <u>Green Onions & Peppercorns</u> or <u>Raspberry Vinegar</u>
- $^1/_3$ cup olive oil
- I tablespoon finely chopped fresh parsley

Put sliced mushrooms into a large glass jar or bowl. Mix rest of ingredients, choosing vinegar variety for taste desired. Pour over mushrooms. Refrigerate overnight and drain before serving.

HONEY DRESSING

Such a simple name for such an extraordinarily good dressing! It adds sparkle to your fruit salads. (Remember that honey is not advisable for children under two.)

$2/3$ cup granulated sugar, optional
I teaspoon dry mustard
I teaspoon paprika
I teaspoon celery seed
$1/3$ cup honey, warmed to make it easy to mix
5 tablespoons <u>Raspberry</u>, <u>Chive</u>, <u>Peach</u> or <u>Sweet Onions Vinegar</u>
I teaspoon grated onion
I cup salad oil, part olive oil
$1/2$ teaspoon salt
$1/4$ teaspoon pepper

In a blender combine sugar, mustard, paprika, celery seed, honey, vinegar and onion. Add oil slowly, drop by drop, while running blender at low speed. Add seasonings to taste, then chill several hours before using.

POPPYSEED HONEY DRESSING

Wonderful with fresh fruit salads or spinach salad.   MAKES ABOUT 2 CUPS

$^1/_2$ cup granulated sugar

I teaspoon dry mustard

I teaspoon celery seed

I teaspoon poppyseeds

dash salt

$^1/_3$ cup honey

$^1/_3$ cup any fruit or berry flavored <u>Vinegar</u>

I cup vegetable oil

Mix sugar, spices and salt in a bowl; pour into a blender. Add honey and vinegar, running blender on low setting until well mixed. Add oil slowly with blender on low. Chill before using.

CHINESE GINGER SALAD DRESSING

Leafy lettuce topped with this piquant dressing makes a delightful introduction to an Oriental feast.

I medium onion, chopped into small pieces

I medium carrot, peeled and diced

I stalk of celery, diced

I cup <u>Mixed Herbs & Spice</u> (with ginger root), Peppers & Spice (with ginger root) or <u>Green Onions Vinegar</u>

I teaspoon minced fresh peeled ginger root or
$^1/_2$ teaspoon ground ginger

I cup oil (part olive oil, if desired)

$^1/_2$ cup soy sauce

I small tomato, diced

salt and pepper to taste

Place all ingredients in a blender and process on high speed until smooth. Store in refrigerator.

TIP: You may add a dash of cayenne pepper for a hotter flavor.

SOUTH OF THE BORDER AVOCADO DRESSING

Excellent served over cold cooked vegetables atop a bed of greens. MAKES ABOUT 2 CUPS

   1 large or 2 small avocados, peeled and diced
   1 clove garlic
   $^1/_4$ teaspoon cayenne pepper
   dash dry mustard
   $^1/_4$ teaspoon chili powder
   $^1/_2$ cup plain yogurt
   $^1/_2$ cup mayonnaise
   $^1/_4$ cup sour cream
   $^1/_4$ cup <u>Garlic</u> or <u>Green Peppers Vinegar</u>
   1 medium tomato, seeded and diced, if desired
   green onions, for garnish
   sour cream, for garnish

Combine all ingredients, except the tomato and garnishes, and whiz in a blender until well mixed. Stir in tomato, if desired, and top with thinly sliced green onions and a dab of sour cream.

BONNE FEMME VINAIGRETTE

This basic salad dressing has many variations, depending upon your choice of vinegars.   MAKE ABOUT ²/3 CUP

    1 tablespoon mustard, homemade or any Dijon-style*
    3 tablespoons any flavored Vinegar
    ¹/2 cup salad oil, part olive, if desired
    fresh herbs, if desired
    salt and pepper to taste

Combine mustard and vinegar in a small bowl. Add oil slowly, while whisking. You may add your favorite herbs to enhance the vinegar flavor. Adjust seasoning with salt and fresh-ground pepper.

VARIATION
Experiment by adding tomato juice, mayonnaise or yogurt, minced garlic or shallots, crumbled bleu cheese or sour cream to this basic recipe.

*For delectable homemade mustards, see *Gourmet Mustards: The How-Tos of Making & Cooking with Mustards* by Helene Sawyer and Cheryl Long. Dijon-style is a classic.

RASPBERRY COOLER

Oddly, this drink is not at all sour. Simply mellow and more full-bodied than regular pop. Experiment with herb vinegars for a refreshing change from iced tea.

Makes 1 serving

> 1 to 2 tablespoons <u>Raspberry</u> or other <u>Vinegar</u>
> ice cubes to fill tall glass
> 7-Up, sparkling water or ginger ale

Place vinegar in a tall glass, add ice cubes and fill with 7-Up, sparkling water or ginger ale. Stir and enjoy! Sugar may be added if you use sparkling water.

TIP: If using one of the herb vinegars, garnish with a fresh sprig of that herb, for example, mint leaves or parsley.

RED HOT CHILI SAUCE

When barbecuing meats and chicken, add this nippy sauce during the last 20 minutes of cooking.　　　　　　　　　　　　　　　　　　　　　Makes 5 cups

　　I green bell pepper, seeded and diced
　　I fresh red hot chili*, seeded and diced, or I teaspoon chili powder
　　2 (15-ounce) cans stewed tomatoes
　　I medium onion, chopped
　　2 cloves garlic, minced
　　¹/4 cup olive oil
　　4 tablespoons fresh chopped parsley
　　2 tablespoons honey
　　2 tablespoons brown sugar
　　2 teaspoons salt
　　I teaspoon fresh ground pepper
　　¹/4 cup Chives & Chili, Garlic, Blackberry or Peppers & Spice Vinegar

Combine all ingredients in a large saucepan and cook over low heat for about 45 minutes, stirring frequently. Blend in food processor or blender until smooth. Store in covered jar and refrigerate.

*VARIATION

For those who don't like it hot, substitute a mild yellow or green pepper for the red hot chili pepper.

GARLIC BARBECUE SAUCE

Great over ribs or chicken!   Makes about 2 cups

    1 (6-ounce) can tomato paste
    1 1/2 cups water
    3 tablespoons <u>Garlic Vinegar</u>
    2 tablespoons mustard
    2 tablespoons brown sugar or honey
    1 teaspoon salt
    1/2 teaspoon pepper
    1 clove of garlic, minced, optional

Combine all ingredients in a small saucepan. Simmer 20 minutes, stirring often.

SWEET & SOUR SAUCE

Pour over fried chicken wings or deep-fried fish fillets for an Oriental treat. Serve with rice and a marinated cucumber salad.   Makes about 2 cups

    2 tablespoons cornstarch
    1 (15 1/4-ounce) can pineapple chunks
    1 green, red or yellow bell pepper, seeded and diced
    1/3 cup <u>Orange</u>, <u>Cherry</u>, <u>Garlic</u>, <u>Chives & Chili</u> or <u>Cranberry Vinegar</u>
    1/2 cup brown sugar
    2 tablespoons soy sauce

Mix cornstarch with a little water. Combine all ingredients in saucepan. Cook until thickened, stirring constantly, about 5 minutes over medium heat.

EASY PINK SAUCE

This recipe is so easy I'm almost embarrassed to include it. But this book wouldn't be complete without my old standby. Delicious over salads, raw or cooked vegetables, Crab or Shrimp Louis. Makes about ¹/2 cup

> ¹/2 cup mayonnaise
>
> 4 teaspoons <u>Raspberry</u> or other dark red fruit <u>Vinegar</u>,
>   such as <u>Blackberry</u> or <u>Blueberry</u>
>
> honey or sugar to sweeten, as desired

Combine all ingredients, stirring well. Refrigerate.

VARIATION

Substitute sour cream or yogurt for mayonnaise.

SWEET HOT MUSTARD SAUCE

Team this very special mustard with a bottle of your best vinegar for a perfect gift!

4 ounces dry mustard

1 cup <u>Raspberry</u>, <u>Mixed Herbs & Spice</u>, <u>Tangerine & Cinnamon</u> or <u>Lime Vinegar</u>

2 eggs

1 cup granulated sugar

$^1/_4$ teaspoon salt

1 $^1/_2$ cups mayonnaise

1 tablespoon grated lime peel or grated orange peel, optional

Mix mustard and vinegar in glass bowl and let stand, covered, overnight. Beat in eggs, sugar and salt. Cook in top of double boiler, stirring until thick. Cool. Add mayonnaise and beat well. Store in refrigerator. Use within 3 weeks.

HOMEMADE MUSTARD

A classic that makes a special gift.   MAKES ABOUT 2 CUPS

4 ounces dry mustard (I prefer Coleman's)

2 tablespoons sweet white wine

2 eggs, well-beaten

$^1/_2$ to 1 cup <u>Raspberry</u>, <u>Lime</u>, <u>Dilled Garlic</u> or <u>Apricot with Allspice</u> <u>Vinegar</u>

1 cup granulated sugar

Combine all ingredients, stirring well. Store in refrigerator.

COOKING WITH VINEGARS • Sauces and Mustards   **73**

LIME MARINADE

Marinate firm white fish fillets before grilling over hot coals. Also delicious with fresh vegetables.   MAKES ABOUT 1 1/2 CUPS

> 1/3 cup Lime Vinegar
> 1 teaspoon salt
> 1/2 cup salad oil, part olive
> 1 small lime, thinly sliced
> 1/2 cup white wine
> 2 tablespoons fresh parsley, chopped

Combine all ingredients in small deep bowl, beating until well blended. Marinate fish or vegetables in refrigerator for several hours before grilling.

SHALLOT MARINADE

Create exciting, yet easy vegetable salads with this marinade. Or tenderize less expensive cuts of meat such as round steak by marinating 3 to 4 hours in refrigerator; then broil or barbecue.   MAKES ABOUT 1 3/4 CUPS

> 3/4 cup salad oil, part olive oil
> 3/4 cup Shallot or other Vinegar of choice
> 3 tablespoons shallots, finely chopped
> 1 tablespoon fresh parsley or basil, finely chopped
> 1 teaspoon salt
> 1/2 teaspoon ground black pepper

Mix all ingredients in small deep bowl, beating until well blended.

OREGON CRANBERRY CHUTNEY

*A beautiful red spicy chutney, perfect with roast meats, cream cheese or crackers. This recipe is featured on my bottles of **Oregon Cranberry Vinegar**. I can't recall the number of times someone has asked me at a demonstration where they could buy this wonderful chutney! You can make it yourself very easily, using any variety of vinegar you prefer.*   MAKES ABOUT 7 CUPS

    I cup Cranberry Vinegar
    2 cups sugar
    2 teaspoons ground ginger
    I teaspoon ground cloves
    $^1/_4$ teaspoon chili powder
    5 to 6 drops hot pepper sauce
    I teaspoon salt
    2 garlic cloves, minced
    2 cups whole cranberries, ground in blender with part
       of vinegar for liquid
    3 to 4 medium tart apples, peeled, cored and diced
    I cup chopped nuts (almonds, pecans or walnuts)

Mix all ingredients except apples and nuts in large stainless steel pot with lid. Heat to boiling, stirring constantly, then add apples. Simmer 30 minutes or until thick, stirring occasionally. Add nuts and cool. Store in refrigerator for up to 4 weeks or freeze up to 6 months.

PAPAYA CHUTNEY

Delicious and exotic with roasted meats or fried rice dishes. Also good on sandwiches and hamburgers. Mix with cream cheese for an exceptional spread on nut breads or crackers. MAKES ABOUT 6 CUPS

- 1 cup <u>Mint with Clove</u>, <u>Peppers & Spice</u> or <u>Apricot with Allspice Vinegar</u>
- 1 1/2 cups granulated sugar
- 1 teaspoon ground allspice
- 1 teaspoon ground cloves
- 1 teaspoon salt
- 7 to 8 cups peeled cubed papaya
- 1 hot green chili pepper, seeded and chopped
- 1 clove garlic, minced
- 1 1/2 tablespoons peeled ginger root, finely chopped
- 1 cup seedless raisins
- 1/4 cup chopped toasted almonds, optional

Boil vinegar and sugar together in stainless steel or enamel pot. Add spices and cook 5 minutes. Add papaya, pepper, garlic, ginger, raisins and almonds. Simmer until thick, about 20 minutes, stirring frequently to prevent scorching. Pour into hot clean jars and seal. Process for 10 minutes in a hot water bath.

PETER'S PICKLED PEPPERS

Here is a gourmet gift that's guaranteed to please: beautiful jars of red, green and yellow peppers.
MAKES 1 QUART

  4 green bell peppers
  4 red bell peppers
  4 yellow sweet peppers
  1 cup small onions, peeled
  3 cups <u>Hot Peppers</u>, <u>Peppers & Spice</u> or <u>Lemon Vinegar</u>
  1 cup salad oil, preferably part olive oil
  1 tablespoon salt or salt substitute

Wash and seed peppers. Chop peppers and onions into large pieces. Put vinegar, oil and salt into an enamel or stainless steel pot. Bring to a boil; then add peppers and onions. Cook 6 to 7 minutes. Remove from heat; cool. Store in jars in refrigerator a week before eating. Keeps 1 month, refrigerated.

SPECIAL BREAD & BUTTER PICKLES

Select your favorite vinegar to make these all-purpose pickles.   Makes about 6 quarts

> 6 quarts medium cucumbers, sliced
> 6 medium sweet onions, sliced
> 1 cup salt
> 1 1/2 quarts <u>Chives & Chili</u>, <u>Shallot</u>, <u>Garlic</u>, <u>Dilled Onion</u> or
>   <u>Mixed Herbs & Spice Vinegar</u>
> 6 cups granulated sugar
> 1/2 cup mustard seed
> 2 tablespoons celery seed
> 1 tablespoon whole green peppercorns
> 6 drops Tabasco Sauce

Put sliced cucumbers and onions into large crock with salt. Let stand 3 hours. Place in colander. Drain liquid and rinse away extra salt with cold water. Combine all other ingredients and boil in large stainless steel or enamel pot, adding cucumbers and onions a few at a time. Simmer 4 to 5 minutes, stirring gently, then pack into clean jars and seal. Process in hot water bath 15 minutes.

PEPPER-FLAVORED PICCALILLI

If you ever have a summer like we do here in Oregon where tomatoes stay green until the snow falls, try this recipe to use them up. Save a few jars, if you can, for holiday presents.   MAKES ABOUT 8 QUARTS

> 25 to 30 pounds green tomatoes, diced
> 1 dozen large sweet onions, peeled and chopped
> 1 cup salt
> 2 quarts plain white vinegar
> 2 quarts water, divided
> 2 1/2 quarts Green Peppers or Chives & Chili Vinegar
> 6 pounds granulated sugar
> 4 to 6 tablespoons whole pickling spices

Place tomatoes and onions in large bowl, sprinkle with salt and let stand overnight. Next morning, strain tomatoes and onions in colander. Place in large stainless steel or enamel pot, then add the 2 quarts plain white vinegar and 1 quart of the water. Boil slowly for 45 minutes. Strain again and return to kettle, adding the flavored vinegar, 1 quart water, sugar and spices. Bring to a boil, reduce heat and simmer slowly for 1 1/2 hours, stirring frequently. Pour into clean jars, seal and process in hot water bath 15 minutes.

About the Author

*M*arsha Peters Johnson founded and operated the firm, Oregon's Own Gourmet Vinegars, specializing in the production of a wide range of flavors. Together with her husband, Paul, she produced thousands of bottles each year. Marsha and Paul have two sons and a daughter.

Acknowledgments

*T*o the three fine women who made this project even imaginable: Cheryl Long, Heather Kibbey and Cynthia Fischborn. Special thanks to my vinegar-loving husband and family for their capacity to eat my home-cooked experiments. And lastly, to my children, for sleeping soundly while I wrote.

INDEX

COOKING WITH VINEGARS 29

APPETIZERS

BEVERAGES

CHUTNEYS

DRESSINGS

ENTRÉES

CREATIVE COOKING SERIES
for Gift-Giving & Flavorful Cooking

Order these delightful how-to cookbooks now! Create stunning gifts from your kitchen and dazzle friends and family with new taste combinations. Techniques from the experts. Here's what to do with garden bounty: herbs, vegetables, berries, fruits and even flowers. Hard-to-find recipes and simple-to-use methods. Capture summer's abundance and enjoy all year long!

GOURMET MUSTARDS: The How-Tos of Making & Cooking with Mustards
HELENE SAWYER AND CHERYL LONG

A must for your pantry! For creative gift-giving and entertaining. Over 125 recipes starring mustard in all its marvelous variety.   ISBN 1-889531-04-9   116 pages $7.95

CLASSIC LIQUEURS: The Art of Making & Cooking with Liqueurs
CHERYL LONG AND HEATHER KIBBEY

Award-winning book showcasing recipes for the famous, hard-to-find and traditional liqueur recipes. Easy instructions yield fabulous results.   ISBN 0-914667-11-4   128 pages $9.95

GOURMET VINEGARS: The How-Tos of Making & Cooking with Vinegars
MARSHA PETERS JOHNSON

A classic! Learn the secrets to creating chef-quality flavored vinegars using fruits, flowers, herbs, spices and veggies. Superb recipes.   ISBN 1-889531-05-7   84 pages $6.95

Discover other intriguing titles from Sibyl Publications:

FOOD NO MATTER WHAT! Stories & Recipes for Perfect Dining in an Imperfect World

TAKING CHARGE: Caring Discipline That Works at Home and at School

SACRED MYTHS: Stories of World Religions

To Order:

SIBYL Publications • 1007 S.W. Westwood Drive • Portland, OR 97239 • (503) 293-8391 • email: ms@sibylbooks.com

Call 1-800-240-8566

Visit our web site for all of our titles: www.sibylbooks.com